THE U.S. ARMY

THE U.S. ARMY

BY HENRY I. KURTZ

Defending Our Country
The Millbrook Press
Brookfield, Connecticut

Cover photos courtesy of: AP/Wide World (top left, middle, bottom right, bottom left); Marv Wolf/FPG International (top right); seal courtesy of U.S. Army. Illustration on p. 35 by Sharon Lane Holm.

Photos courtesy of: New York Public Library Picture Collection: pp. 8, 39, 42, 46; Wide World Photos: pp. 11, 25, 28–29, 48, 54; U.S. Army: pp. 13, 21, 23, 27 (both), 32, 34, 49, 57; FPG International: pp. 15 (Jeffrey Sylvester), 36 (Michael Nelson); USAF: p. 18; The Bettmann Archive: p. 45; National Archives: p. 51.

Library of Congress Cataloging-in-Publication Data
Kurtz, Henry I.
The United States Army / by Henry I. Kurtz.
p. cm.—(Defending our country)
Includes bibliographical references and index.
Summary: Surveys the history, role, organization, combat units, and weapons of the United States Army.
ISBN 1-56294-242-5 (lib. bdg.)
1. United States. Army—Juvenile literature. [1. United States. Army.] I. Title. II. Series.
UA23.K83 1993
355'.00973—dc20 92-12660 CIP AC

Published by The Millbrook Press
2 Old New Milford Road, Brookfield, Connecticut 06804

★ ★ ★

CONTENTS

I

INTRODUCTION: FROM TRENTON TO THE PERSIAN GULF

The sound of gunfire shattered the early morning silence as hundreds of American Continental Infantry swarmed into the British-held town of Trenton, New Jersey. It was dawn on the morning of December 26, 1776, and the American Revolutionary War was well into its second year of fighting. General George Washington had boldly led his tattered, half-starved troops across the Delaware River. His plan was to stage a surprise attack on the British stronghold at Trenton.

Washington counted on the British and their German allies (called Hessians) being off guard on the day after Christmas. He was right. Sluggish from too much food and drink, the British and German troops stumbled sleepy-eyed and groggy out of their quarters to meet the American attack. Cheering loudly, the American troops advanced, firing their muzzle-loading muskets. Cannoneers fired their brass-barreled cannon, sending grapeshot (clusters of small metal balls) into the dense ranks of the enemy. The fighting was furious. A British counterattack was beaten back, and the British commander was killed by American sharpshooters.

In 1776, the American victory at the Battle of Trenton
marked a turning point in the Revolutionary War.

Soon the British and Hessian troops found themselves sur-
rounded. With all avenues of escape blocked, they surrendered. More
than 900 British and Hessian soldiers were taken prisoner; another 120
were killed or wounded. Only four Americans had been wounded during the battle. Two others had frozen to death during the frigid night
march.

As General Washington surveyed the scene of victory, he exclaimed to one of his officers, ''This is a glorious day for our country.'' And indeed it was. The winter of 1776 was the low point of the American Revolution. The American Army had suffered several defeats and had shrunk to a few thousand men. But the victory at Trenton, and the one at Princeton eight days later, revived hope. It brought fresh volunteers to fill the thinning ranks. And it saved the infant American Army just as it seemed on the verge of collapse.

More than two hundred years later, on the hot desert sands of the Middle East, a far larger and more powerful American Army found itself battling to save another small nation from losing its independence. This time the place was the tiny oil-rich kingdom of Kuwait, on the Persian Gulf. On August 2, 1990, Kuwait's much larger neighbor Iraq—with an army of over one million men—launched an attack on the smaller country. In a matter of days Iraq had swallowed up its Arab neighbor. But the Iraqi victory was only temporary.

The United States quickly forged a coalition of Arab, African, European, Latin American, and other countries opposed to Iraqi aggression. The United States moved more than 400,000 troops into the troubled region. They included elite units like the 1st Cavalry Division and the 82nd and 101st Airborne divisions.

The Iraqis, however, refused to withdraw from Kuwait. The United States and its allies then launched Operation Desert Storm, beginning a massive air attack on Iraqi military targets. The U.S. Army played a key role in this early phase of the Persian Gulf War. Sleek AH-64 Apache attack helicopters based in Saudi Arabia flew across the border into Iraq. Flying at high speed and low altitude—and without lights—the choppers launched a devastating attack on Iraqi radar stations. Coming in on their targets, the Apaches unleashed laser-guided Hellfire missiles. Then they opened up with volleys of 70mm Hydra rockets and 30mm cannon fire. The mission was a success. With the radar stations knocked out, coalition aircraft could fly undetected against targets deep inside Iraq.

For five weeks, coalition air attacks softened up the enemy. Then, on February 24, 1991, a four-day lightning ground attack was launched against the Iraqi Army. American soldiers led the swift-moving armored columns that smashed through the Iraqi defenses. They were a far cry from their brothers-in-arms in the American Revolution. The soldiers of 1776 carried smoothbore muskets, which could be fired only two or three times a minute. The modern American soldier carries a rapid-fire M-16 rifle that can unleash thirty rounds in a matter of seconds.

Even more awesome were the high-tech weapons systems employed by the U.S. Army during Operation Desert Storm. The Army's MLRS (Multiple Launch Rocket System) can fire as many as twelve powerful rockets at a time, hitting targets as far off as 20 miles (32 kilometers). The ultramodern M1A1 Abrams tank—the U.S. Army's main battle tank—has laser-directed, computer-operated 120mm cannon. Its night-vision sights can penetrate the thickest smoke and dust clouds, enabling pinpoint accuracy when firing at an enemy tank.

The American soldier of today goes into battle with personal body armor—helmet and flak vest. He has modern rapid-fire small arms and artillery. And he is given air cover by jet fighters and attack helicopters. Without a doubt, the American soldier is the best-protected and most heavily armed fighting man in history. Little wonder that only one hundred hours were needed to win the ground war against Saddam Hussein's Iraqi Army. It took Washington and his Continental Army seven years to beat the British in the Revolutionary War. By contrast, it took less than seven weeks for U.S. and coalition forces to win the Persian Gulf War.

In the Persian Gulf War of 1991, American soliders led a lightning ground attack that smashed Iraqi defenses. Here troops from the 82nd Airborne Division take part in a desert drill in the weeks before the war broke out.

★ ★ ★

WHAT THE ARMY DOES
AND HOW IT DOES IT

The technology of war has changed greatly since the early days of the U.S. Army. But the Army's primary mission hasn't changed all that much. First and foremost, the Army has the job of defending the United States against an attack by a foreign aggressor. Because the United States is a global power, the U.S. Army must be ready to fight overseas when necessary to uphold U.S. national and international interests. The Army's job in wartime is to carry out land operations in support of U.S. policy and interests.

The Army also has important peacetime functions as well. It must maintain combat readiness through intensive training. In case of natural disasters, such as floods and forest fires, Army forces may be used in disaster relief efforts. The Army may also be called upon to put down civil disturbances when local police forces are unable to control the situation. Under the direction of the Army Corps of Engineers, it carries out projects to improve river and harbor facilities and to control floods.

★ Leading the Army

The United States Army is one of the three major departments that make up the Department of Defense. The others are the Department of the Navy and the Department of the Air Force. Of the three branches of the service, the Army is the oldest and the largest in terms of manpower. The secretary of defense is the civilian head of the Department of Defense and a member of the president's Cabinet. He reports directly to the president, who is commander in chief of all the armed services.

The Department of the Army can be thought of as a pyramid. At the top, or pinnacle, is the secretary of the Army, a civilian official appointed by the president. He has overall responsibility for managing the Army—from the training of its soldiers and the selection of new weapons to its deployment in the field. The secretary's headquarters are at the Pentagon, in Washington, D.C.

The Army seal
carries the motto
"This We'll Defend."

The next level of the pyramid includes both civilian and military officials. On the one hand, the secretary of the Army is assisted by an under secretary and five assistant secretaries. The under secretary is the secretary's chief deputy. The five assistants have responsibility for specific areas, such as financial management, research and development of weapons and equipment, and various other crucial activities.

Alongside the Army's secretariat stands the Army Staff. This is a group of experienced military officers headed by the Army chief of staff, who is usually a four-star general. The chief of staff is also a member of the Joint Chiefs of Staff, a group whose other members include the chief of naval operations, the Air Force chief of staff, and the commandant of the U.S. Marine Corps. In time of war, the Joint Chiefs of Staff plan and supervise combat operations.

Under the Army chief of staff is the Army's General Staff of senior officers. It is their job to run the Army's general operations and day-to-day functions. Another group, the Special Staff, has the job of supervising Army bureaus with highly specialized and technical functions. The surgeon general, who is the Army's chief medical officer; the judge advocate general, who is in charge of all legal matters; the chief of the National Guard Bureau, which oversees the military forces of the fifty states; and the chief of the Army Reserve forces are all part of the Special Staff.

★ Army Commands

Below the command structure, on the next level of the pyramid, are the various Army commands. A ''command'' in Army talk is a collection of units, with appropriate equipment and personnel, headed by a commander. Most Army commands come under the heading of CONUS, which is an abbreviation for Continental United States. Some of the major commands of CONUS are described here.

The U.S. Army Forces Command (or FORSCOM) is responsible for maintaining the combat readiness of the six field armies based in the United States. FORSCOM is also responsible for the active and reserve forces stationed in America's overseas possessions—the Commonwealth of Puerto Rico, the U.S. Virgin Islands, and Guam. In short, all Regular Army, National Guard, and Reserve ground forces within the continental limits of the United States and its overseas territories come under this command. FORSCOM has its headquarters at Fort McPherson, Georgia.

Army reservists return to a warm welcome after the Persian Gulf War. The Reserves play an important role in the modern Army.

SPEAKING ARMY LANGUAGE

You say . . .	The Army says . . . .
air defense artillery soldier	duck hunter
Air Force	zoomies
armor soldier	treadhead
artillery soldier	cannon cocker
bathroom	latrine
broken down	deadlined
correct	squared away
engine	power pack
exercise	PT (physical training)
first sergeant	top
gossip	poop
headquarters	head shed
helicopter	chopper
infantryman	grunt
Marines	jarheads
National Guardsmen	weekend warriors
Navy	squids
Pentagon	puzzle palace
rifle	bullet launcher
room/dormitory	barracks
soldier	troop or GI
stop	hold
supplies	beans 'n bullets
undercover police car	K-car
yes	check
late night/early morning	o'dark thirty

The U.S. Army Training and Doctrine Command (TRADOC) is in charge of Army training programs, specialized schools, and other educational activities. It also supervises the Army Reserve Office Training Corps (ROTC) programs at high schools and colleges. TRADOC has its headquarters at Fort Monroe, Virginia.

Getting supplies and equipment to Army personnel is the job of the U.S. Army Matériel Command, which is based in Alexandria, Virginia. Across the Potomac, at its headquarters in Washington, D.C., the U.S. Army Corps of Engineers plans and puts into operation various military and civilian projects. Intelligence gathering is in the hands of the U.S. Army Intelligence and Security Command. Medical services and hospitals are provided by the Army's Health Services Command, based at Fort Sam Houston, Texas. The Criminal Investigation Command carries out investigations of criminal activities wherever U.S. troops are stationed. And the Military District of Washington Command is in charge of all military activities in and around Washington, D.C. The Military Traffic Management Command manages cargo and personnel transportation and overseas shipping for the Army, as well as for the Department of Defense as a whole.

There are also Army commands that handle U.S. troops stationed abroad. These include the U.S. Army, Europe (based in Germany); and the U.S. Army, Pacific (headquarters in Hawaii), which manages all U.S. forces in Hawaii, Japan, and other Pacific regions. It works closely with the Eighth U.S. Army, stationed in Korea.

Finally, the Army has some highly specialized commands with specific wartime as well as peacetime functions. One of the more glamorous of these is the 1st Special Operations Command at Fort Bragg, North Carolina. The elite Special Forces units, trained for counterguerrilla warfare and operations behind enemy lines, are supervised from here. So are the Army's three Ranger battalions, highly mobile units that can strike by land, sea, or air.

An infantry soldier with an M-16 rifle.

★ ★ ★

COMBAT UNITS AND WEAPONS

The U.S. Army has three components. First is the Regular Army, which is made up of men and women who have volunteered for full-time military service. In recent years, the Regular Army has numbered about 740,000 men and women. Supporting the Regular Army in wartime are the two reserve components: the U.S. Army Reserve and the Army National Guard.

The U.S. Army Reserve is under the direct control of the federal government. Army National Guard troops are under the control of state governments except when mustered into federal service in wartime or other national emergencies. There are over 3,500 National Guard units in the fifty states, with about 400,000 soldiers. The Army Reserve has about 250,000 troops. The Active Army, at any given time, consists of the Regular Army and any reservists who are on active duty.

The Army has several combat branches. The infantry are troops trained to fight on foot or from armored vehicles. The armored branch consists of troops in tanks or armored personnel carriers. Artillery and air defense artillery consist of soldiers who handle large cannons and launchers that fire rockets and missiles. Army aviation consists mainly of attack and transport helicopters, along with some light reconnaissance planes. Special forces are elite troops who carry out operations deep in enemy territory. And combat engineer units work closely with advancing infantry and armor units.

Supporting the combat branches (or arms) are a variety of combat support units. Among these are military intelligence, transportation, and quartermaster corps units. All of these specialized units provide vital services to the combat troops, from trucking supplies and ammunition to the front lines to setting up field kitchens and field hospitals to provide hot meals and proper medical care to the combat soldiers.

The modern Army places great stress on rapid movement and heavy fire power. This is easily seen in the fact that of the Regular Army's eighteen active divisions, six are mechanized and four (including the 1st Cavalry) are armored. Two others, the famed 82nd and 101st Airborne Divisions, are designated as airborne. But only the 82nd still uses parachute landing attacks. The 101st is now an airborne assault division that uses helicopters to deploy its troops.

The basic fighting unit in the field is the battalion. It is usually referred to as a maneuver battalion because its job is to maneuver, or move from point to point to pin down and fight enemy forces. Each battalion consists of smaller units. These units are called companies in the infantry, batteries in the artillery, and troops (or companies) in armored battalions.

Companies are subdivided into platoons, and platoons into squads. In the field, a typical light infantry squad consists of two four-man fire teams. During a firefight, one team provides covering fire, while the other maneuvers against the enemy position. Usually they will leapfrog—the first team covers while the second advances; then the second team covers and the first advances.

★ Infantry Weapons

A typical infantry squad will be armed with the M16 rifle with a thirty-round magazine. One member of the team, called a grenadier, will have an M203 grenade launcher, which attaches to the M16. Other squad members may carry a squad automatic weapon (SAW). This weapon is a 5.56mm light machine gun with a 200-round ammo belt.

Soldiers from the 101st Airborne Division operate a 105mm howitzer in Saudi Arabia.

Sometimes a squad member will have the heavier 7.62mm M60 machine gun. Noncoms usually carry a .45-caliber pistol along with other weapons.

Infantry companies also have special squads equipped with heavier weapons. Among these are the M224 60mm mortar. It can provide advancing infantry with supporting fire by hurling its shells almost 2 miles (3 kilometers). To knock out enemy tanks, infantry units can employ the M47 Dragon Medium Antitank Missile System. The missile is launched from a disposable tube, which can easily be handled by a single soldier. The Dragon can disable an enemy tank at a distance of over ½ mile (0.8 kilometer).

Faced with attacking enemy helicopters, infantry units can bring into play a small portable air defense weapon called the Stinger Anti-Aircraft Missile System. The weapon consists of a single round in a tube that can be hand-held and fired while propped on an infantry-man's shoulder.

★ Armored Vehicles

The old image of foot-slogging infantry soldiers with full packs and weapons having to hike for miles to get into a battle zone is pretty much a thing of the past. Highly mobile mechanized divisions are the backbone of today's Army. So today's modern infantry is more likely to ride into the fighting zone in an armored vehicle. The most high tech of these modern war chariots is the M2 Bradley Fighting Vehicle. The Bradley is part tank and part fortress on wheels. From its tanklike turret sprouts a 25mm rapid-fire cannon and a 7.62mm machine gun. It also has six firing ports from which light machine guns can be fired. And it carries a tank-killing TOW missile launcher. (TOW stands for tube-launched, optically-tracked, and wire-guided.) A nine-man infan-

HOW SOLDIERS SEE AT NIGHT

A soldier who can see at night has a great advantage over one who cannot. The Army has several devices that allow soldiers to see even on a moonless night. One of these, called Night Vision Goggles, is strapped to the soldier's head. He can use the goggles in combat or for map reading, driving a vehicle, or even first aid.

THE NIGHT VISION GOGGLES USED BY GROUND FORCES.

Another device, called the Aviator's Night Vision Imaging System, is attached to an Army helicopter pilot's helmet. He uses this system at night when flying close to the ground to avoid detection by the enemy. He can see the ground and enemy forces, but they can't see him. Another device, the Individual Served Weapon Sight, is mounted on rifles, machine guns, and rocket and grenade launchers and is used during combat.

Some of the Army's night-vision devices use lasers or heat to intensify, or strengthen, images at night. Others use beams of infrared light.

try squad can fight from inside the vehicle. Or the squad can dismount to attack enemy infantry under cover of the Bradley's heavier guns. The M3 Bradley Cavalry Vehicle is a smaller version of the M2.

When it comes to transporting troops, the mainstay of most mechanized and armored divisions is the M113A2 and A3 series of Armored Personnel Carriers. Armed only with a .50-caliber machine gun, this vehicle can transport an eleven-man rifle squad. Variations of this armored vehicle are used to carry everything from cargo to air defense missiles and smoke generators (used to create smoke screens to cover the movements of advancing infantry and armor).

What gives punch to an infantry attack are its tank-dominated armored divisions. U.S. armored divisions use three main battle tanks. Heading the list are the M1 Abrams Main Battle Tank and the newer, more sophisticated M1A1 and M1A2. The M1 has a 105mm cannon, along with a .50 caliber and two 7.62mm machine guns. The M1A1 sports a more powerful 120mm gun. The newer model Abrams also have a system of protective devices and heavier armor plating. With this protection, they can withstand attacks by nuclear, chemical, and biological weapons.

The M60A3 and M48A5 Patton Main Battle Tanks are mainly used by Reserve forces, including the National Guard.

★ Artillery and Missiles

Artillery support is an essential part of ground warfare. The modern Army employs a wide range of field guns to support advancing infantry and to defend against enemy attacks. Cannon are either towed by truck or are mounted on tracked vehicles—so-called self-propelled guns.

The mainstays of the Army's field artillery are the M102S 105mm and the M119 105mm towed howitzers. Both are operated by seven-

A column of M1A1 Abrams tanks on the move in Kuwait.

man crews and have effective ranges of up to 8 miles (13 kilometers). For a heavier wallop, the Army has 155mm howitzers, which come in either towed or self-propelled models. They are capable of hitting targets at 10 miles (16 kilometers) or more. Various types of shells can be used, including conventional explosive types or those with nuclear warheads. A laser-guided shell called a Copperhead can knock out an enemy tank at a distance of 10 miles (16 kilometers). The latest in the conventional arsenal of cannon is the 203mm self-propelled howitzer mounted on a tracked vehicle. It can lob a shell nearly 15 miles (24 kilometers).

Today's artillery includes something even more powerful—the guided missile. Two types of missiles are employed by the Army: surface to surface and surface (or ground) to air. The first of these is used to knock out enemy troops and armor. The Lance Battlefield Support Missile is mounted on a tracked vehicle. Its shells can be armed with conventional or nuclear payloads, and its range is 60 miles (75 kilometers).

For defense against enemy aircraft, the Army uses a variety of air defense missiles. One of these is the Chaparral AD Missile System, which employs Sidewinder missiles. The HAWK AD Missile System can hurl radar-guided missiles nearly 25 miles (40 kilometers).

Probably the best known of the Army's ground-to-air missiles, thanks to the Persian Gulf War, is the Patriot AD Missile System. Many deadly Iraqi Scud missiles aimed at Saudi Arabia and Israel were knocked out by the radar-guided Patriots.

Top: The Army's 155mm self-propelled howitzer.
Bottom: A Patriot missile leaves its launcher.

★ Aircraft

Finally, Army aviation plays a vital role in modern warfare. Some helicopters are used to transport troops and equipment to the battlefield. The UH-60A Blackhawk helicopter, for example, can transport an infantry squad or haul a small vehicle to a battle zone. The larger cargo helicopters, such as the CH-47D Chinook, can airlift tons of supplies or larger pieces of equipment—for example a 155mm howitzer—to where they are needed.

Attack helicopters seek out and destroy enemy infantry and armor—as well as other vital targets. The Army's two main attack hel-

Apache helicopter gunships on patrol in Saudi Arabia.

icopters are the AH-64A Apache and the AH-1 Cobra. The deadliest of these is the Apache. Its impressive arsenal of weapons includes a 30mm "chain gun" cannon and a mix of anti-armor Hellfire missiles and 2.75-inch rockets. The laser-directed Hellfires can knock out a tank from a distance of nearly 4 miles (6 kilometers). The Cobra also has a deadly bite. This helicopter gunship roars in on an enemy position with its three-barrel 20mm cannon firing rapid bursts. It can also unleash nearly forty Hydra 70 rockets and eight TOW tank-killing missiles.

The Army also employs some fixed-wing aircraft. For the most part, these are used on scouting and observation missions. Army aviators may fly their planes close enough to enemy positions to guide artillery and missile fire. They can provide commanders with on-the-spot reports of enemy troop movements and can take aerial photos of fortifications and supply depots.

IV

★ ★ ★

MEN AND WOMEN
OF THE ARMY

Today's U.S. Army is made up of men and women who have volunteered for military service. Since the end of the Vietnam War and the military draft in the 1970s, efforts have been made to attract qualified people to the Army. Most enlisted men and women are high school graduates. Nearly all officers are college graduates, and many have postgraduate degrees.

Up until World War II, women were not permitted to serve in the Army. That changed in 1943 with the creation of the Women's Army Corps (WAC). However, women soldiers remained a separate part of the Army and performed relatively few specialized tasks until 1978. In that year, the Women's Army Corps was disbanded and WACs became soldiers equal to their male counterparts. Today more than 80,000 women serve in the Army. Women are represented in more than 300 of the nearly 370 military occupation specialties and nearly all of the more than 200 commissioned officer specialties. There are women helicopter pilots and women generals commanding large units

with mostly male soldiers. There has been discussion about allowing women to serve in combat. But at the present time, female soldiers do not serve in the combat arms—infantry, armor, and special forces.

Soldiering remains as it has always been, a hard profession. Certainly, there are risks of personal danger in time of war. The hours are often long, especially when units go out on maneuvers or during times of national emergency. But there are the rewards of service to one's country, good pay, and benefits. There also are educational opportunities to learn skills that are useful in civilian life. As it has throughout its long history, the Army is ready to live up to its motto: "This We'll Defend."

★ Enlisted Personnel

Enlisted men and women form the largest group in the Army. They include the lowest-ranking privates and specialists, as well as noncommissioned officers (corporals and sergeants), or NCOs. NCOs command small units or perform certain special jobs.

Anyone between the ages of seventeen and thirty-five who meets certain basic requirements can enlist in the Army. Newly enlisted soldiers must go through basic training. During this eight-week period, the soldier is taught basic drill, how to handle standard infantry weapons (such as the rifle, bayonet, and grenade), survival techniques in the field, and other fundamentals.

Although women do not serve in combat, they are represented in more than three hundred occupation specialities.

Hard physical training is part of Army life.

From basic training the soldier moves on to AIT (advanced individual training). What training the soldier gets depends on his or her MOS (military occupation specialty). Specialized schools are located on Army posts all over the United States. Here, soldiers are taught how to drive a tank, operate missile systems, or run a post newspaper. Some advanced training lasts a few weeks, but some specialties require months of training. Once training is complete, the soldier is posted to a unit in the United States or an overseas base.

U.S. ARMY RANKS AND INSIGNIA

Commissioned Officers *(lowest to highest)*

Rank

| Second lieutenant | First lieutenant | Captain | Major | Lieutenant colonel | Colonel |

Brigadier general   Major general   Lieutenant general   General   General of the Army

Warrant Officers *(lowest to highest)*

Warrant officer 1   Chief warrant officer 2   Chief warrant officer 3   Chief warrant officer 4

Enlisted Personnel *(lowest to highest)*

Private (E-2)   Private first class   Corporal   Specialist four   Sergeant   Staff sergeant

Sergeant first class   Master sergeant   First sergeant   Sergeant major   Command sergeant major   Sergeant major of the Army

Because of the important role noncommissioned officers play in maintaining discipline and combat readiness, special emphasis is placed on NCO training. The motto of the NCO Development Program is "Training Is Sergeants' Business." A sergeant must go through a series of special courses that may last most of his or her Army career.

★ Officers

Higher command functions are in the hands of commissioned officers—officers who hold the ranks of lieutenant on up to general. Officers may receive their commissions by several routes. Up until the Civil War, the United States Military Academy at West Point provided nearly all the officers of the U.S. Army. Today, most officers are commissioned through the Senior Reserve Officer Training Corps programs at hundreds of American colleges and universities. Officer candidates must complete a four-year ROTC program along with regular college studies. They then receive both a college degree and a commission as second lieutenant.

Only a small percentage of U.S. Army officers now come from West Point. But this military academy still provides the most rigorous officer training program. Some NCOs may get commissions through Officer Candidate Schools. Another small group—such as doctors or lawyers—may receive direct commissions because of special skills.

Warrant officers rank below commissioned officers but higher than noncoms. Usually they are former NCOs who receive a warrant from the secretary of defense because of special skills they possess. Many Army helicopter pilots are warrant officers. Others work in technical areas such as electronics, computers, and military intelligence.

West Point cadets receive the Army's most rigorous officer training.

THE ARMY
THEN AND NOW

The earliest American soldiers were members of colonial militia units. All of the original thirteen American colonies had militia units made up of all men of arms-bearing age—usually sixteen to sixty. These militias were mainly used to fight against hostile Indians. During the French and Indian War, militiamen fought alongside regular British troops against French Canadian troops.

As the American colonies developed, the colonists began to think of themselves as Americans rather than British subjects. They objected to heavy taxes imposed on them by a British Parliament in which they had no direct representation. Hostilities broke out when British regulars clashed with American militiamen on April 19, 1775, first on Lexington Green and later at Concord's North Bridge. Using Indian-style hit-and-run tactics, the American militiamen drove the British back to Boston and then laid siege to that city. Two months later, on June 14, the American Continental Congress in Philadelphia voted to raise ten companies of riflemen. The date June 14, 1775, is thus considered the birthday of the U.S. Army.

Washington takes command of the
newly formed Continental Army.

The newly formed Continental Army, with General George Washington at its head, was supposed to have 20,000 men and officers in its ranks. But throughout the Revolutionary War its ranks were usually much thinner. Against the Continental Army and colonial militia, Great Britain sent 20,000 British regular troops and 30,000 German mercenaries. The British and German troops were experienced professionals. But they were often outmaneuvered and outfought by the less-experienced but resourceful and determined American soldiers.

Early in the war, the American Army suffered several serious defeats. But the tide began to turn after the American Army's victories at Trenton and Princeton in the winter of 1776–1777. At the end of 1777, American troops under General Horatio Gates won a stunning victory at the Battle of Saratoga. On October 17, British general John Burgoyne surrendered his Army of five thousand men to the victorious Americans.

Several more years of war followed, with British forces steadily losing ground. Finally, at the end of 1781, the main British Army under Lord Cornwallis was trapped at Yorktown, Virginia, by a combined force of American and French troops. Outnumbered and cut off from supplies and reinforcements, Cornwallis surrendered his Army on October 19, 1781, ending the American War of Independence.

The year 1781 also saw the creation of the War Office, which became the Department of War in 1789. Its job was to direct military operations, and it was responsible to the Congress. The head of the department was called secretary at war (later changed to secretary of war). With this arrangement, the Congress was clearly establishing the American tradition of civilian control over the military—a tradition that continues to this day.

With the end of the Revolutionary War, however, the Army was almost completely disbanded. At the time of the U.S. Constitution's adoption in 1788, the Army numbered only 672 enlisted men and 46 officers. The Constitution gave the Congress the power "To declare war . . . To raise and support armies . . . [and] To provide for calling forth the militia to execute the laws of the union, suppress insurrections and repel invasions." The president, however, was designated as head of the armed forces, or "commander in chief."

So the Constitution divided power over the military. The president and the secretary of war, who was a member of the president's Cabinet, had direct control over the Army and Navy. They could order them into battle once war was declared. But only the Congress could declare war. And it was the Congress that had the power to decide on the size of the Army and to provide the money needed to pay and equip those troops. Americans were fearful that a large regular (or standing) army would be a threat to democracy. So the regular Army was deliberately kept small. Up until World War I, the main reliance was on volunteers and the state militias in time of war.

In the years immediately after the War of Independence, the Army's primary role was to protect settlers on the western frontier against Indian attacks. But the new nation soon came into conflict with Great Britain again. During the early 1800s, British ships stopped American merchant vessels on the high seas and forcibly seized (impressed) American seamen for service on British warships.

Americans were outraged by this practice, and Congress declared war on Great Britain on June 18, 1812. When the War of 1812 broke out, the regular Army had fewer than seven thousand men. By contrast, the British had one of the largest armies and the most powerful navy in the world. Fortunately, the British had their hands full—they were at war with the French emperor Napoleon. On the American side, thousands of militiamen and other volunteers flocked to the colors, adding strength to the regular Army.

The record of the American Army in the War of 1812 was a mixed one. Often the less-experienced American soldiers were no match for the battle-hardened British troops and were defeated. But in some battles, the Americans fought gallantly and successfully. And in 1815, a mixed force of volunteers and militia under General Andrew Jackson defeated a British Army at the Battle of New Orleans. This battle actually took place two weeks after a peace treaty had been signed, but neither the Americans nor the British at New Orleans knew of it.

Andrew Jackson led American troops at the Battle of New Orleans.

With the end of the War of 1812, the Army went back to peacetime duties. As the frontier expanded westward, it was often the Army that blazed a trail. U.S. regulars built roads and bridges, and Army posts were often the first settlements in new territories. There were hard-fought campaigns against Chief Black Hawk's Sauk Indians in the West and the Seminoles under Osceola in Florida.

Westward expansion also brought the United States into conflict with Mexico. As Americans settled in Texas and California, there was pressure to make these territories part of the United States. Although Texas proclaimed its independence from Mexico in 1836, friction continued between Mexico and the Republic of Texas. Skirmishes between U.S. and Mexican troops along the Texas-Mexico border led to an American declaration of war in the spring of 1846. Only 8,000 strong when war began, the Army expanded to over 100,000 men. Only 30,000 of these were regular troops. The rest were short-term volunteers recruited by the states.

The Mexican Army was trained along European lines, and it had several years of combat experience. The U.S. Army was smaller than the Mexican Army. But it was better organized, its soldiers were better equipped and trained, and it had a more professional corps of officers. The result was a string of American victories. While General Zachary Taylor moved south into Mexico from Texas, General Winfield Scott landed another American Army at Veracruz and marched on Mexico City. Other U.S. troops took control of the Mexican provinces of California, New Mexico, and Arizona. The capture of Mexico City brought the war to an end, and a peace treaty was signed in February of 1848. The Mexican War was the first time in its history that the U.S. Army fought a full-scale war on foreign soil.

Soon, war clouds were gathering again. Northern and Southern states were coming into conflict over the issue of slavery and the related issue of whether a state could secede, or withdraw, from the Union. The issue came to a head after the election of President Abraham Lincoln. Believing Lincoln would move to abolish slavery, eleven Southern states withdrew from the Union and formed the Confederate States of America. When the U.S. government tried to send supplies to Fort Sumter in Charleston, South Carolina, Confederate troops bombarded the fort. The attack on Fort Sumter, on April 12, 1861, was the start of the American Civil War. It would prove to be the bloodiest war in American history.

The U.S. Army numbered only 16,000 at the outbreak of the Civil War. By war's end, some two million men had enlisted or had been drafted into the U.S. (Union) Army. This army reached a peak strength of about one million men in 1865. Most of the men served in volunteer regiments recruited by the various states.

The Civil War was a war of firsts. For the first time, the U.S. government enacted a military draft law. All able-bodied men up to the age of forty-five had to register and be prepared to serve in the Army if called. For the first time, extensive use was made of military railroads to transport men and supplies. The telegraph became an important means of battlefield communication. New weapons included more powerful rifled cannon, breech-loading rifles, and an early form of the machine gun called the Gatling Gun. Toward the end of the war, many Union soldiers were armed with seven-shot repeating carbines and the fifteen-shot Henry rifle—which Confederate soldiers dubbed ''that infernal machine the Yankees load up on Sunday and fire all week.'' The U.S. Army even had its first aerial force— an observation balloon corps useful in spying on enemy troop movements.

The war also saw the first major employment of black soldiers in the U.S. Army. Nearly 190,000 African Americans fought to preserve the Union and abolish slavery.

Black troops played an important part in the Union
victory in the Civil War. This unit was photographed
in 1865, just before the end of the war.

The Civil War resulted in the greatest loss of lives in any of the
wars this country has fought. Over 600,000 Union and Confederate
soldiers died. Under tough commanders like Ulysses S. Grant and
William T. Sherman, the U.S. Army waged total war, destroying cities and laying waste to rich farmlands. The hard-handed strategy worked.
Outnumbered Confederate armies under generals Robert E. Lee and
Joseph Johnston surrendered in the spring of 1865, bringing the war
to an end.

Union general
Ulysses S. Grant.

One of the important lessons of the Civil War was the value of a well-trained professional officer corps. Many opponents of the U.S. Military Academy at West Point, founded by President Thomas Jefferson in 1802, argued that it was elitist and antidemocratic. But the war proved its value. Nearly all of the U.S. Army's top military commanders in the Civil War were graduates of West Point.

From 1865 until the end of the 1800s, the U.S. Army found itself again pushing Indians farther westward to make room for newly arrived settlers. There were bloody conflicts with the Plains Indian tribes—the Sioux, Cheyennes, Kiowas, and others. During one of these campaigns, Lieutenant Colonel George A. Custer, who had won fame during the Civil War, was defeated by a combined force of Sioux and Cheyenne Indians at the Battle of the Little Bighorn. Custer and five companies of the 7th U.S. Cavalry were wiped out to the last man.

The Indian conflicts came to a bloody end in 1890 at Wounded Knee, in an incident in which more than 150 Sioux—including many women and children—were killed. Controversy still surrounds this final clash between the Army and the Indians, which many regard as a black mark on the Army's record.

The Army also fought another foreign war as the century drew to a close. When a U.S. battleship mysteriously blew up in the harbor of Havana, Cuba, the U.S. declared war on Spain, which then ruled the Caribbean island. Harsh Spanish rule had led to a Cuban revolt, which many Americans supported. Others saw an opportunity to acquire overseas territories, as European powers had done. Once again, as in the Mexican War, a small professional army supported by volunteers proved its worth in the field.

Despite many flaws in its organization, equipment, and command structure, the Army won a string of victories over Spanish troops in Cuba and the Philippines. Because of its short duration and low casualties, the war against Spain has been called "the Splendid Little War."

As a colonel during the Spanish-American War, Theodore
Roosevelt led a cavalry unit called the Rough Riders.

The Army saw little serious military action over the next twenty
years. However, innovations and improvements continued. In 1907 the
Army's Signal Corps set up an aviation unit—the forerunner of the
Army Air Corps, which lasted through World War II, and the later
separate U.S. Air Force (established in 1947).

America tried to remain neutral in World War I, which began in
Europe in 1914. But Germany's use of unrestricted submarine warfare
resulted in the deaths of many Americans traveling on a British ship,
the *Lusitania*, sunk by a German U-boat (submarine). A German plot
to encourage Mexico to go to war with the United States was also
uncovered. As a result, Congress declared war on Germany and its

allies in 1917. Aided by a military draft law (covering young men from twenty-one to thirty years of age), the Army rapidly expanded from 213,000 men in federal service in 1917 to over 3,500,000 one year later.

Some 2,000,000 U.S. Army troops actually served overseas in the American Expeditionary Force headed by General John "Black Jack" Pershing. The arrival of these fresh troops helped to turn the tide of battle in favor of the Allied forces of France and Great Britain. In the final German offensive in 1918, American troops played a significant role in the battles of the Meuse-Argonne and St.-Mihiel, which resulted in Germany's defeat.

The arrival of U.S. troops in Europe helped bring the Allied victory in World War I.

By the time of the armistice in November 1918, the U.S. Army had become well-schooled in trench warfare and the use of airplanes and tanks in support of attacking infantry. But within two years after the victorious American Army returned from Europe, it had been reduced to only 230,000. Throughout the peaceful years of the 1920s and 1930s, the Army's strength was under 150,000. Except for the creation of the Army Air Corps in 1926 as a separate arm of the service, little was done to modernize the Army before World War II.

Meanwhile, in Europe, Hitler's Nazi movement came to power in Germany and Mussolini's fascists took control in Italy. In Asia, Japan used military force to gain control of portions of China. Even after Germany's invasion of Poland in 1939, which touched off World War II, American public opinion favored neutrality. But the Japanese air attack on the U.S. naval base at Pearl Harbor on December 7, 1941, plunged the United States into the war. Japan's Axis allies, Germany and Italy, declared war on the United States a few days later. The United States now found itself facing a war on two fronts—in the Pacific and in Europe. In what became the greatest military mobilization in American history, the U.S. Army went from 269,000 troops in 1940 to over 8,000,000 men and women in 1945.

From 1941 to 1945, the Army found itself fighting in every type of terrain. American troops fought in the hot deserts of North Africa. They battled in the rugged mountain regions of Italy. And they fought in the steamy jungles of South Pacific islands. Fighting alongside their British, French, Chinese, and other Allies, American troops drove Hitler's legions out of North Africa, Sicily, and Italy. In the Pacific, troops led by General Douglas MacArthur helped drive the Japanese back to their home islands. For the first time in history, air forces played a major role in war. The U.S. Army Air Corps, using B-17

World War II saw fighting on two fronts,
Europe and the Pacific. Here, U.S. troops land
on the Pacific island of Rendova in 1943.

Flying Fortresses and B-24 Liberators, launched massive bombing attacks against German and Japanese industrial centers and troop concentrations.

In June of 1944, American and other Allied troops staged the greatest amphibious attack of all time, landing over 200,000 troops at Normandy on the coast of France. Using airborne infantry units to parachute behind enemy lines and tank columns to punch through the German defenses, the American and Allied forces liberated Paris and drove the Nazi Army across the Rhine into Germany. At the same time, the Russian Army invaded Germany from the east. On May 7, 1945, Germany surrendered.

Japan continued to fight on, however. President Harry Truman was faced with the possibility of mounting a large-scale invasion of Japan. He feared that this would cost many thousands of American lives. As a result, he decided to use a new and devastating weapon— the atomic bomb. In August of 1945, Army Air Corps bombers dropped the first (and only) atomic bombs used in warfare on the Japanese cities of Hiroshima and Nagasaki. Japan surrendered immediately, and World War II was over.

But a new threat had emerged, that of Communism expansion. With it came what became known as the Cold War. This was a period of tension between the Western democracies and the Communist nations of Eastern Europe (led by the Soviet Union) and those of Asia (led by China). Because of the possibility that the Cold War might heat up into a real war, the United States now maintained a larger army than ever before in its history. Throughout the remaining years of the 1940s, the Army had about 600,000 soldiers.

The National Security Act of 1947 brought all the services together under the Department of Defense, with headquarters in the vast Pentagon building in Washington, D.C. What had been the War Department now became the Department of the Army. Additional legislation in 1950 gave the secretary of the Army greater operational control over the Army. He was also given the right to make basic policy changes without Congress having to pass a law each time.

One major change that occurred during this period was an end to Army units segregated by race. From the Civil War until just after World War II, African American soldiers fought in all-black units, usually commanded by white officers. President Harry Truman ordered an end to this practice in 1948. Since that time all U.S. Army units have been racially integrated.

In 1950 the Cold War heated up when Communist North Korean troops invaded South Korea. The Soviet Union and Communist China backed North Korea, while the United States and its allies supported South Korea. The United States sent in American troops to hold back the invading North Koreans. It also urged the United Nations to send a multinational force to stem Communist aggression. In all, some sixteen nations provided combat troops for the United Nations army that fought against the North Korean and Communist Chinese forces. The U.S. Army, however, provided the bulk of the ground troops. The war dragged on for three years. Neither side won a decisive victory, but the United States and its allies did prevent a Communist takeover of South Korea.

As a major world power, the United States maintained large military forces all around the globe. Most U.S. Army forces stationed overseas were based in Europe—mainly in Germany. Backed by U.S. nuclear power, the U.S. Army served as a shield against a possible invasion of Western Europe by the Soviet Union and its Communist bloc allies. Emphasis was placed on conventional warfare in which ground troops backed by artillery and tanks would fight the kind of classic land battles that had been seen in World War II.

U.S. paratroopers search for snipers
in Vietnam. The helicopters that landed
them can be seen in the background.

But the next war the United States became involved in was highly
unconventional. The Vietnam War proved to be one of the longest and
least popular in American history. After World War II, political and
religious differences resulted in Vietnam (a former French colony) being
divided into the Communist-controlled north and the Western-oriented
south. To prevent a Communist takeover of the entire country, the

United States began sending military advisers to South Vietnam in the late 1950s.

American involvement increased in the 1960s as the war heated up. Trained to fight a conventional war, the U.S. Army now found itself in rugged jungle terrain fighting against an elusive guerrilla army—the Communist Viet Cong. The United States attempted to counter the enemy's hit-and-run tactics with antiguerrilla Special Forces units, the Green Berets. The Army also used helicopter assault forces to stage swift strikes against suspected Viet Cong and North Vietnamese strongholds.

As the war seemed to go on endlessly and American casualties mounted, antiwar sentiment in the United States grew. Finally, in 1973, the United States withdrew its forces. For the first time in American history, the U.S. Army pulled out of a war without having won a clear-cut victory or having accomplished its main goal.

Army commanders learned many lessons in Vietnam, and in its aftermath (and with the end of the military draft in 1973) many changes were made. Tougher training and morale-building programs were introduced to create a higher degree of professionalism in what was now an all-volunteer army. Military units were made more efficient and new weapons systems were introduced. The Army also beefed up its elite Ranger battalions and Delta Force commando units for use in smaller brushfire wars.

Opportunities to test out the new Army came in Grenada and in Panama. In 1983 the government of the tiny Caribbean island of Grenada was overthrown by leftist rebels with ties to Communist Cuba. Other nations in the region called for U.S. intervention. U.S. Army Rangers, along with marines and Navy SEALS (an elite commando unit), invaded Grenada on October 25, 1983. Despite some mishaps, the five-day campaign resulted in the toppling of the pro-Communist government.

The U.S. Army went into action again in the final days of 1989, this time in the Central American country of Panama. There, General Manuel Noriega had proclaimed himself dictator. He ousted democratically elected officials and announced that his country was in a state of war with the United States. A combined U.S. Army, Navy, Air Force, and Marine strike force, numbering some 12,000, was sent to join an equal number of U.S. troops already stationed in the U.S.-controlled Panama Canal Zone to oust Noriega and restore democratic government. The Panamanian forces were quickly subdued, and Noriega surrendered on January 3, 1990. He was brought to the United States to stand trial on drug-smuggling charges. (He was convicted in 1992.)

Grenada and Panama were proving grounds for new U.S. military tactics and equipment. The lessons learned in these minor actions proved invaluable when the U.S. Army was sent to liberate Kuwait in the 1991 Persian Gulf War. Also, many of the soldiers—especially among the officers and noncommissioned officers—who participated in Operation Desert Storm had gained valuable combat experience in the earlier operations.

The victories in Grenada, Panama, and the Persian Gulf restored the confidence and morale lost during the Vietnam War period. Operation Desert Storm also proved that the modern U.S. Army is an efficient, hard-hitting fighting force that can be rapidly deployed anywhere in the world.

A U.S. Army captain holds a Kuwaiti child, who waves her country's flag. American forces played a leading role in the Allied offensive that restored Kuwait's government in 1991.

By 1992 the Cold War seemed to be at an end. Communism had collapsed in Eastern Europe, and the Soviet Union had broken up into separate republics. Today, the U.S. Army faces new challenges. Instead of a major conventional war, Army commanders see a greater likelihood of brushfire wars requiring rapid deployment of well-trained, streamlined, and fast-moving units. Whatever the future may hold, the U.S. Army's role will remain the same as it has been for two hundred years—to defend the nation and its interests, and to preserve the peace by being ready for war.

★ ★ ★

IMPORTANT EVENTS
IN ARMY HISTORY

1775	The first American army, called the Continental Army, is formed by the Continental Congress to fight in the Revolutionary War.
1783	The Revolutionary War ends, with the Continental Army victorious.
1789	The War Department is established to direct military affairs.
1802	The U.S. Military Academy opens at West Point, New York.
1812– 1814	The U.S. Army fights the British during the War of 1812; General Andrew Jackson defeats the British at the Battle of New Orleans after the war is officially ended.
1846– 1848	In the Mexican War, the U.S. Army, in its first full-scale war on foreign soil, defeats the Mexican Army.
1861– 1865	The U.S. (Union) Army reaches a peak strength of about one million men during the Civil War; Congress passes (1863) the United States' first draft law.

1898	During the Spanish-American War, the U.S. Army defeats Spanish forces in Cuba and the Philippines.
1903	The Army creates a General Staff system and sets up the office of chief of staff.
1916	Under the National Defense Act, the Army is divided into the Regular Army, Volunteer Army, Organized Reserves, and National Guard.
1917–1918	During World War I, two million American soldiers serve overseas in the American Expeditionary Force, helping defeat Germany and its Allies.
1941–1945	The United States Army fights in World War II after Japan attacks Pearl Harbor; the first atomic bomb, developed by Army and civilian scientists, is dropped (1945) on Hiroshima, Japan.
1950–1953	During the Korean War, U.S. Army forces in Korea reach a peak strength of nearly 500,000.
1965	The first U.S. Army troops are sent to Vietnam.
1973	All U.S. combat troops withdraw from Vietnam after a cease-fire is signed; an all-volunteer Army is established.
1976	Women are admitted to the U.S. Military Academy for the first time.
1983	Operation Urgent Fury is conducted in Grenada, in the Caribbean.
1989	Operation Just Cause is conducted in Panama, in Central America.
1991	U.S. Army troops take part in Operation Desert Storm in the Persian Gulf.

BOOKS FOR
FURTHER READING

Judith Hemming, *Why Do Wars Happen?* New York: Franklin Watts, Inc., 1988.

Ian Hogg, *Tanks and Armored Vehicles.* New York: Franklin Watts, Inc., 1984.

Elaine Landau, *Chemical and Biological Warfare.* New York: Dutton Children's Books, 1991.

J. Nicholaus, *Main Battle Tanks.* Vero Beach, FL: Rourke Corp., 1989.

Carl P. White, *Citizen Soldier: Opportunities in the Reserves.* New York: Rosen Publishing Group, 1990.

Brian Williams, *War and Weapons.* New York: Random House, 1987.

INDEX